THE
POWER
OF
KNOWING
YOU

To Sue & Amy,
Best wishes
Shel

Learning from the past

Sheila McMahon

THE POWER OF KNOWING YOU
Learning from the past

Published by Sheila McMahon

Copyright © 2015 Sheila McMahon

contact@mindmanagementforyou.com

www.mindmanagementforyou.com

Copy Editor: Colette Bratton

Cover design: Stuart Maddox Design & Rocket Ink Ltd

Photographer: John McMahon

Interior Design & Typesetting: Tanya Bäck

ISBN: 978-0-9932138-0-9

Contents

The Power Of Knowing You
Learning from the past

In an ideal world all children would be brought up with unconditional love.[1] They would be shown unconditional love, both physical and emotional, whilst being supported, encouraged and given the confidence needed to become their own person. They would be provided with healthy boundaries, protected until adulthood or adolescence and then taught how to be responsible for themselves to grow as individual adults.

Parents do their best. A lot of the time they learn from their parents and trust that this is the way to do it. Often parents, when they themselves were growing up, were not allowed to question their own parents behaviour and were conditioned[2] into thinking they had no choice but to copy it. If the behaviour came from a place of fear, judgement, criticism and expectation it may leave devastating effects on a child who might grow up to believe they are not good enough, not lovable and not understand why.

---

1. John Bowlby 'Attachment theory'
2. Rogers 'conditions of worth'

I was one of these children. I went into therapy in my mid-twenties. I found out that what I thought was normal wasn't, and that I blamed myself for things that were out of my control and were not actually my fault. I learned that I was a self-sabotager.

I continued to self-sabotage until, through my therapeutic journey, I became aware of where my childhood had gone wrong and why I continued to self-sabotage.

Why I wrote this book

In my experience of working as a counsellor, I see time and time again how negative conditioning from the past holds people back from doing what they want, and prevents them from being who they want to be. Your past can unlock the answers to what behaviours are limiting your present and jeopardising your future.

When you become aware of why you do the things you do, you can then choose to keep the positive stuff, throw out the negative and allow yourself to be who you want to be and achieve what you want to achieve.

I'll never forget one of my clients having a lightbulb moment and saying out loud:

"How can I know what I want until I know who I am?"

You can lose sight of who you are for many reasons. Sometimes you may get caught up in social norms, going along with other people's expectations and you may feel a loss of identity.

Sometimes, through no fault of your own, you may not have had the emotional support and encouragement to grow an identity in the first place! You can be living the life that some else believes is the right life for you. You may feel it is the right path and you may be happy doing this. However, you may feel less satisfied and as a result you may feel helpless and out of control, as you have been directed by outside influences and not by you.

This book has practical exercises to help you reflect on your life so far. To explore past experiences, your behaviour and the behaviour of others around you. To help you build awareness of how your past experiences have affected you. To explore who you truly are and what matters to you so you can live your life through your values and beliefs.

'In my experience, when you build a solid foundation of who you are as a person, the confidence naturally shines through.'

I also wrote this book for personal reasons. When I was seven I wanted to end my life. Now, as a counsellor, I wanted to understand why the seven year old me was even thinking about suicide. I didn't have the internet back then so I couldn't find out how to kill myself. It's scary to think that if the information had been readily available on how to commit suicide, the likelihood is I would have done it. I wanted to understand why I felt so bad as a child when, from the outside, it looked like everything was normal.

I was diagnosed with depression in my twenties, and after having counselling I naively thought '*That's it, I'm fixed for life*', but the symptoms of my depression kept coming back. As the depression wouldn't permanently go away, I wanted to find out what was really behind it.

In this book I disclose a lot about my past, to show how negative conditioning and past physical and mental abuse can prevent someone from living the life they want to live.

Preface

At the start of the book I tell my story from how I saw my world as a child. I do this to highlight how a child does not see their world as an adult does. I was not able to rationalise what was going on, and as a result I blamed myself for my experiences. In this book I have highlighted personal thoughts in single quotation marks. I have highlighted quotes in double quotation marks.

Throughout the book I give examples of my own learning and awareness. These are highlighted in the grey areas.

As part of the research for this book I interviewed members of my family, friends and clients. These interviews and research are also highlighted in the grey areas.

I use vancouver referencing to highlight certain words, their origins and links to further information.

The exercise boxes within this book are for you. These are exercises to help you reflect on your life, so you can gain more insight into your foundation and your unconscious beliefs. This may help you to become aware of any negative beliefs and self-limitations that might be preventing you from living the life you want.

In my experience, when you build a solid foundation of what matters to you, you trust in your ability. You accept that sometimes you will get it wrong and that there is no such thing as perfect. You can feel good about yourself, and things should not feel so personal anymore. You may see things from a different perspective so you can treat yourself as your own best friend, and that's when the transformation happens! If you don't believe me, keep reading.....

My story from a child's point of view

Once upon a time there was a little girl who grew up on a farm in the West of Ireland. She had three older brothers, two of whom bullied her for her entire childhood. One of them made her stand in front of the mirror and tell herself how ugly and fat she was, so she believed from a young age that she was ugly and fat. They used her for their amusement and mentally and physically abused her. She tried to tell her parents how she was feeling. Initially they told her brothers off but after a while she was told to "just ignore them". Through her parents' rejection when she asked for help, she learned that her opinions did not matter. She learned that support was not an option.

To try and make it stop, at seven years of age she got a knife, went up to her brothers and desperately said: "Do you want me to kill myself?". They laughed in her face and she wished she had the courage to stab herself dead.

The bullying was non-stop. She was born with a cleft palate and took speech lessons but she felt ridiculed by the speech teacher. Most things she owned, her brothers either broke or took away from her, and as a result she believed she didn't deserve to own anything.

She was made to do the chores around the house whilst her brothers played because she was a girl. She was taught that men were better than women and that a woman was expected to put the man's needs first. She watched her mother's misery and struggle. She learned that her life would also be a struggle.

Her mum was busy working and was emotionally unattached. As a result, this girl thought she was not loved and therefore believed she was unlovable. Her dad was a hardworking man who was often angry. She loved the fun times she spent with him. When her parents went out she would beg her dad not to go and leave her at home with her brothers. When he went out, she felt abandoned.

She saw love as conditional, confusing and not consistent.

The only thing that kept her going was her belief and faith in God. She cherished the idea that someone loved her and accepted her for who she was. She would chat to him regularly. When she was eight she prayed that she would die. She couldn't see what her purpose was on earth and wanted to be with someone who loved her.

As the years went past she became more anxious. She never knew what mood her dad would be in and she became fearful of him. She was told that if she ever got pregnant she would be disowned by the family. She lived in fear, isolation, frustration and felt worthless.

Her father enjoyed amateur dramatics. He wrote and put on a play for the neighbours and she performed a part in the play. She loved it. She had fun. She knew from that moment she wanted to be an entertainer.

She went to secondary school. She couldn't understand why boys would try and speak to her because she believed she was ugly and fat. She thought:

'I am so ugly that I can't understand why people don't get sick by looking at me.'

In her final year in school she got to experience a drama class and loved it. Once again, she felt that entertaining was something she could do.

She went to a performing arts college in Dublin to study acting. Her first year was good as she made friends and started to build her confidence. However, her cleft palate and a medical condition she was unaware of meant she couldn't do the vocal exercises, and as a result was told that she was lazy.

At acting college she was never given a speaking part, and was told that unless she lost her accent she would never be an entertainer. She hit rock bottom. She could not see the point of her life and wanted it to end.

Then, by chance she got a speaking part in a play. She went home, looked in the mirror and had a life-changing moment. She said:

"I'm Sheila McMahon and nobody is ever going to walk all over me again."

She realised:

'I am no better than anyone else, but
no-one is better than me.'

She concentrated on her work and by the end of the year delivered a great performance.

She went on to teach drama and dance to children. When it came to the end of year show, she wrote the play herself to ensure every child had a speaking part. After six years of teaching she wanted to do more. She wanted to be a famous actress. She was told that she needed to enrol in a prestige school to further her career but soon realised she had already done the required training at college. She decided to set up her own theatre company and create her own work.

Someone suggested she try stand-up comedy. The idea terrified her, but excited her too. She thought:

'I can't do that' - but there was a voice
inside her saying, 'why not?'

She booked herself into the biggest comedy venue in the Republic of Ireland, performed her first stand-up gig as a character called 'Auntie Betty' and she was in ecstasy. The feeling of achievement was out of this world - she had done it!

As time went by, she struggled doing stand-up as she felt a personal rejection if people didn't laugh at some of her jokes, but she continued gigging.

In her mid-twenties she started to have panic attacks and was told by her doctor she was depressed. She wanted to know why, so she went into therapy. After a painful process of offloading pain and anger, she realised her parents did love her, but they didn't know how to show it unconditionally. She learned that her parents showed her their love in practical and financial ways, but were not able to give her the consistent, emotional love she needed.

Up until this time she could not sustain a long term relationship. She would often meet men who would end up bullying her, but she didn't know why this was happening. She always ended her relationships. She had learned from a young age that love wasn't consistent, so she would reject them before they could reject her.

This became a regular pattern. She knew she had the potential to be great. One day she decided she'd had enough of feeling suppressed so moved to the UK to make a fresh start.

She stuck a pin in the middle of a UK map and moved to Banbury. Her mother went with her to help her find a job and a place to live. When her mother left, she sat in a bed and breakfast, not knowing anyone, absolutely petrified thinking about what she'd done. She realised she had choices.

> **'I can sit here and allow the fear and anxiety to get worse, or I can acknowledge it's a beautiful day, pick up my guitar, go down to the local park, sing at the top of my voice and see what happens.'**

And that's what she did. Regardless of how scared she was, she loved to entertain. By the end of the day she had a crowd of people around her, amazed by her story and received two offers to join bands. That was a life changing day for her. She knew she'd made the right decision to put herself out there and to trust that life could be better for her. She knew she was going to be fine.

Today

Today I am who I want to be and where I want to be. I work half my week as a counsellor and the other half performing stand-up comedy and music. If something gets in my way I do something about it. If I'm depressed I accept it because I know it will pass. I don't let depression get the better of me! I am no longer the victim of my experiences.

I am now with a lovely partner who treats me the way I deserve to be treated. The difference is that I value myself, and live by my morals and values. I am with him because I want to be with him, not because I need to be with him. Each day I am filled with excitement and hope about the future. If I died today I would be very proud and happy with what I have achieved. I am my own best friend. Today, and with each gift of a new day I am free to be me. By learning from my past, accepting it and allowing myself to grow, I have empowered myself to let my inner light shine through. This is what I call, the power of knowing you.

Caution

Depending on where you are with your own life right now, some of you may be able to do the suggested exercises and apply them to make positive changes to your life straight away. If you don't feel able, this could be because of deep-rooted conditioning and suppressed emotions. These exercises will help give you a deeper awareness of where you are at present.

If you have good intention, but can't seem to consistently do things that make you happy, there could be self-sabotaging going on. If this is the case, I encourage you to work with a professional counsellor to uncover the deep-rooted issues that are holding you back. Yes, it can be painful, but it is so worth it. In chapter 20 about counselling support you will find information on finding a qualified counsellor.

For the moment, I encourage you to try the exercises in the book and enjoy exploring who you are!

CHAPTER 1

Awareness

Who are you?

Seems like a simple question doesn't it?

Sometimes a person can get so caught up in life that they can forget about themselves and feel their priority is to please other people. As a result they may not be aware of their own needs.

Let's break this down. The 'who' in who you are is the biggest part! It makes up the whole of you as a person, and I bet there are a lot of different aspects to you.

Your morals, values and beliefs

Let's explore your morals, values and beliefs. These are your set of rules that you like to live your life by. If you don't have any, then this is an opportunity to think about what is important to you as a person. For example, I often hear people say 'treat others the way you want to be treated'. I agree with this and I also believe in treating yourself the way you want to be treated!

Initially, your morals, values and beliefs may have been formed by the people who influenced you or who you grew up with. People who care about you sometimes believe they know what is best for you, and that you'll have a happier, more fulfilling life if you do what they say and what they want you to do.

However, if what they want you to do doesn't feel right to you and it's not what you want, then this can lead to you feeling out of control as a result of living your life through other people's beliefs instead of your own.

Some influences can come from your parents, school, friends, media, society and religion. Who and what have influenced you?

So what are your own beliefs? Here are some questions to help you explore what matters to you.

Morals, values and beliefs

Think about your morals, values and beliefs. What are they?

What will you not put up with?

If someone close to you was asked to describe your morals, values and beliefs - what would they say?

If someone close to you was asked to describe your morals, values and beliefs, what would you _want them_ to say?

What morals, values and beliefs do you look for in a friend? If you are unsure, what morals, values and beliefs would you like to have in a friend?

Don't worry if you don't know the answers. The fact that you are taking time out to think about this is building awareness about yourself, so the answers will come.

Other people's morals, values and beliefs

As mentioned earlier, a lot of beliefs are passed on directly by the people who influenced you, and their beliefs may have come from the people who influenced them. As we know, time moves on and ideas change. Previous generational beliefs aren't always right today, but some people may be stuck in past generational thinking where beliefs were from a place of control and fear. As time has moved on, we've gained more insight into what is fair, how people should be treated and how to get the best from ourselves and others.

It can be helpful to find out what their beliefs are? Here are some questions to continue exploring this area.

Family values

In thinking about the people you grew up with, what were their morals, values and beliefs?

Are there any statements or sayings that were said to you that as an adult you don't agree with?

Are there any behaviours that you picked up from others that sometimes make you question, 'Why do I do that?'

Are there any beliefs that have been passed onto you that you don't agree with?

These exercises will help you become aware of the morals, values and beliefs that have framed your life so far. You can now decide to keep what feels right to you, to learn to let the negatives go and to find out who you truly are.

I encourage you to listen to your gut instinct and to question behaviours and beliefs that might have been projected onto you that don't feel right.

To help you uncover any negative or limiting beliefs, take time to imagine yourself as a child again and think about how you felt.

Memories of when you were a child

How did you view the world? Circle the words that relate to you - exciting, scary, adventurous, overwhelming, confusing? Feel free to put in any other words that come to mind.

How did you see yourself? Valuable, a nuisance, loved, unlovable, rejected, adored, important, special? Again, add any other words that come to mind.

How did you see the people around you? Supportive, better than you, as equals, on a pedestal, helpful, always right, as family / friends, as strangers, loving, kind, caring? Again, add any words that come to mind.

For further exploration circle yes / no / unsure to the following questions:

Your childhood memories continued...

Did you feel listened to as a child?
Yes / No / Unsure

Did you feel that you were compared to other members of your family?
Yes / No / Unsure

Did you feel appreciated as an individual in your own right?
Yes / No / Unsure

Did you feel you were encouraged to find what you were good at?
Yes / No / Unsure

Were you allowed to make your own mistakes?
Yes / No / Unsure

Did you feel loved?
Yes / No / Unsure

Did you feel you were given unconditional love i.e. not judged or criticised?
Yes / No / Unsure

Do you remember being given emotional love e.g. cuddles?
Yes / No / Unsure

Do you remember being told you were loved?
Yes / No / Unsure

What were you proud of as a child?

What frustrated you as a child?

All these questions are to do with a child's needs. Asking these questions helps you to explore whether your needs as a child were met. If they weren't met, it might uncover what was missed in your childhood so you can be aware of your own inner child needs as an adult. Your inner child is the internalised memories, scripts[3] and introjects[4] you carry now from when you were a child. Acknowledging your inner child can unlock certain thoughts and behaviours that you learned as a child and carried into adulthood that might be limiting you. Being aware of any of your needs that were not met as a child gives you the chance to change this, and meet these needs in a healthy way.

> As part of the research for this book I asked my parents what it was like for them as they were growing up. My dad's father unfortunately died when my dad was 11. As a result, his oldest brother was treated as the head of the house. There wasn't much of an age gap between them, so when my father questioned his mum as to why he had to answer to his brother, he was told it was because he was the youngest. My dad is now in his seventies and can still remember being told his opinions didn't matter because he was the youngest in the family. When his oldest brother would make bad decisions (as we all can do at times) my dad was not allowed to question them, and it didn't feel right to him to do things he didn't agree with. As a result, my dad very bravely told me how he had an inferiority complex when he was younger, and still has a bit of it to this day! I'm proud of him for being so honest.

I encourage you to put other people's influences to one side and learn from your past, so you can decide what you want your future beliefs to be!

---

3. Eric Berne 'Transactional Analysis'
4. Carl Rogers 'Person Centred Counselling Theory'

Who are you?

Here are some more questions to help you learn from the past and find out who you are. Try to have fun answering these. In fact, you could allow yourself to be a child and draw the answers to these questions instead? It's whatever works for you! Ask yourself:

Life as a child

As a child I naturally liked to ...

As a child I was curious about ...

As a child I was interested in ...

As a child I lost track of time when I was ...

When I was younger I felt I was good at ...

When I was younger I was told I was good at ...

CHAPTER 2

Achievements

It is important that we acknowledge our achievements.

When I grew up, I was lead to believe that self-praise is no praise. I often hear clients say that their parents would say to them, "Don't be too big for your boots", so they've grown up believing that praising yourself is wrong.

To give an example of this conditioning:

I was on the phone to my dad and he asked me how things were going with my counselling practice. I said: "Great, but because I'm good at what I do I usually have a quick turnaround which means I have to do more networking to let more people know about my services." He said: "Hang on a minute, who told you that you were good?" In the past I would have been saddened by his response and doubted my own ability. I would have read out testimonials from past clients to prove to him that I was good enough. Instead, I said to him, "How can I expect others to believe in me if I don't believe in myself?"

When I am doing stand-up comedy I often have people say to me in a judge-mental way "Are you any good?". I say in a very serious Irish accent: "No I'm shite."…which always gets a laugh. One time I said: "Yes I'm good at what I do" and the person said: "You're full of it aren't you!". The reality is you can't win, and as long as you are alive there will always be somebody criticising you! It is import-ant that you don't take it personally. Often people can't be happy for you because they are not happy with themselves.

The fact is, if I don't believe that I am funny, how can I expect anyone else to!

Praise gets the best out of us as it encourages us to grow. If we don't do it already, we need to be able to praise ourselves and acknowledge our achievements so that when other people praise us we can accept the compliment!

It's important to find a balance between being truthful and being proud of your achievements without coming across as being arrogant. You need to be able to acknowledge your achievements so you can see your capabilities.

Acknowledging your achievements

It can be very easy to focus on what you haven't achieved rather than what you have. Focusing on what you have achieved gives you the motivation and confi-dence to try new things. There is so much to learn from your past achievements – think about what you achieved, how you achieved it, what motivated you and why you did it. All these questions will continue to give you more clarity about who you are as a person and what motivates you.

The following exercise will help you think about what you have achieved. It doesn't matter how big or small the achievement, it could be passing a driving test or having the courage to go for it in the first place! Alternatively it might be passing exams, becoming a parent, getting a job or promotion, travelling or doing something on your own?

Here are some questions to help you think about your achievements:

Achievements

Think of a time when you wanted to achieve something and did. What did you achieve? (This can be as big or as small as you like.)

What actions did you take to achieve this?

What thoughts did you have that helped you to achieve this?

What obstacles did you overcome?

How did you feel after you had achieved it?

I encourage you to make a list of all you have achieved in the past. Thinking about what you have already accomplished can help to remind yourself about your capabilities!

Personally, I keep a portfolio of all my successful gigs and interviews as a record of my entertainment achievements. I've also collected testimonials from counselling clients. If I need a confidence boost, I just look at these to remind myself of what I can achieve and what I'm capable of.

Again, it doesn't matter how big or small your achievements are. It is important you don't self-judge, but instead, allow yourself to acknowledge when you have pushed yourself out of your comfort zone and made it happen!

Achievements

Achievements

This exercise is helping you to build a solid foundation so, if and when unexpected things happen, you have the self-belief to know you can deal with whatever it is in a rational way and carry on.

CHAPTER 3

Conditioning

Conditioning is when you take on the expectations, criticisms and judgements of others.

For example, you could have a parent who believes education is the most important thing and that their child should be focused on this. That is fine if they want to believe this, but often this expectation is put onto the child who may not be as passionate about education as the adult. This may unconsciously lead to the child feeling like a disappointment because they are not living up to the adult's expectations.

> Through conditioning, I learned I got attention and love for what I did, rather than who I was. As a result, I remember being invited to a barbecue and feeling I had to bring my guitar. I remember someone saying to me: "You don't have to bring your guitar", but to me I felt I had to prove my worth by playing songs. It took time for me to believe that bringing myself was enough.

I became aware that I would judge myself on what I did rather than whether I was a good person. Now I have changed this belief, as to me it's more important to be a good person. This is an example of how I now live by my own belief rather than someone else's conditioning.

Sometimes people are conditioned to not speak out about things they don't agree with for fear they might 'create a scene', or bring attention to something that isn't right and therefore they might 'rock the boat'. These are all expressions I have heard in the counselling room and in my life. Sometimes people can try to suppress you, just to keep other people happy and to 'keep you in your place'. This sort of conditioning tends to come from a place of fear and control.

If people have been conditioned not to speak out then sometimes they will encourage you to do the same.

'Sometimes, by following other people's conditioning, you end up conditioning yourself.'

That's why it is important to trust your gut instinct and to voice your opinions. Allow yourself to find the answers that are true to your morals and values as a person.

Conditions of worth[5]

Conditions of worth help you discover how you value yourself as a person. How do you value yourself? Is it by how much money you have? Is it by how good you look? Is it by your status in your job? Is it by how much you own? The danger of valuing your worth by outside influences is that they are often out of your control. For example, if you judge your value by job status, what happens if you lose your job?

I have some clients who are extremely wealthy. They have linked so much of their own self-worth to their money that they are terrified of losing it, and, as a result they feel out of control. They feel the money is controlling them.

Other clients believe the media messages about the importance of looking good. They worry about their looks fading with age, but getting old and having wrinkles doesn't mean you have no value.

It is important to recognise whether you are being directed by outside influences and things that are out of your control, or by your morals and values as a person.

---

5. Carl Rogers 'Conditions of worth'

If you are happy to be directed by outside influences then that is fine – whatever works for you. If not, then I encourage you to look deep inside yourself and find out what really matters to you.

Making comparisons

Making comparisons can very much distort your conditions of worth.

I remember sitting with my dad and him saying: "I'm so lucky because I've got my two daughters here with me", meaning my sister-in-law and I. Then he looked at my sister-in-law and said: "But most importantly, you are the good-looking one."

In my dad's mind he was just making my sister-in-law feel welcome, but in my mind the message was that I am only as good as how I look. If I had let this comment sink in I might have become jealous of my sister-in-law. Making comparisons can easily lead to problems such as jealousy and low self-worth. I know my dad is not aware of the impact of what he says and fortunately I can ignore these sort of comments and see them for what they really are. However, you can imagine how different the impact of these comments would be for someone with low self-worth. We are all individuals with our own strengths that need to be appreciated in their own right, not compared to others.

In thinking about your conditions of worth:

How do you value yourself?

In a therapy session one of my clients talked about a couple she knows that are 'better than her'. When I questioned her about this, she said they were better because they had more money than her, were well spoken and knew how to behave properly with people. She disclosed how the husband of the couple would correct other people if they didn't use proper diction, and would talk down to people to get his own way. She also mentioned that this couple were never affectionate in public.

When I asked her if she agreed with this behaviour, she said: "No, I would never want to talk down to people. I love how my husband and I are loving towards each other."

Further exploration lead to how people would not like being around this couple and how the woman of the couple had voiced to my client how she noticed how much love was in my client's relationship.

It actually turned out that, despite all their wealth and correct diction, they actually were jealous of my client because she was happy in her relationship, not afraid to show physical affection and could just be herself! Through counselling we were able to rationalise her inferiority complex about this couple and see things from a different perspective.

I encourage you to have a think about your conditions of worth? A way to help you think about this is ask yourself:

When it comes to the end of your life, what will you be thinking about?

Will it be the external factors like the car and the house? Will it be the memories you have of the people you love and have loved in your life?

Outside conditioning

When I was in primary school the boys and girls were in separate classes. As a result, boys were like 'aliens' to me! I found it very hard to talk to a boy outside of my family. With my Catholic upbringing I always felt a sense of shame around the opposite sex and an embarrassment around sex and nudity. I was lead to believe it was wrong to spend time with boys because they can get you pregnant. I remember talking to a boy and been scared out of my wits that I was pregnant! When I went to secondary school I was terrified because it was a mixed school, so anytime a boy was near me, I would go red and get very embarrassed.

As an adult now, I believe the outside factors of religious beliefs and having been separated from boys in primary school added to my difficulty talking to boys. If it had been a mixed sex school, and there wasn't such a taboo around sex, the first year of secondary school might not have been so difficult.

CHAPTER 4

Learned Behaviour
And Distorted Connections

As a child I internalised things very differently from how I see them now as an adult. In some cases, children learn from how you make them feel rather than what you say.

Sometimes we may internalise negative behaviour as personal even though it was never intended that way.

For example, my dad felt inferior as a child because he was treated differently being the youngest, and he was told his opinions didn't count. His mum never intended him to feel inferior, and further exploration confirmed she was completely unaware of the impact of her actions.

When I spoke to my oldest brother, I asked him how he saw me as a child when he was growing up. He said he wasn't interested in me because I was the youngest. He found it hard to communicate with me - so he just didn't bother. As a child I internalised his behaviour into feelings of worthlessness and confusion.

It's ironic how my dad and I both experienced the feelings of inferiority because we were the youngest!

> I remember asking my dad questions but, instead of answering me, he would tell me that I was too young to understand. I'm sure he would say the same again to me now if he thought he could get away with it! Whilst I'm able to joke about this, I'm also highlighting how learned behaviour can be passed on unconsciously and without malicious intent.

Often clients disclose in therapy that they were compared to their brother or sister during their childhood. It's sad when siblings are compared against each other as it can have a damaging effect later on in life. It can lead to sadness about missing out on supporting each other and having an equal relationship. Everyone is unique, there is no right or wrong. After all, no-one is perfect!

In thinking about learned behaviour, in Chapter 1 on Awareness, what answer did you put down for:

Are there any behaviours that you picked up from others that sometimes make you question, 'Why do I do that?'

I discovered one recently. Going into town to meet up with a friend, I was automatically going to park in the cheapest car park until I stopped and asked myself, 'why?'. Although it was the cheapest, I've never liked that car park as it is dirty, gloomy and grey!

The place I was meeting my friend had its own car park that was much nicer and brighter, so I asked myself, 'why am I not parking there?'. On reflection, I became aware that I wanted to dedicate every penny to growing my business just as my parents had done. Although money saving like this can be wise, parking in the cheapest car park was ignoring my personal beliefs of 'treat myself the way I want to be treated'. I recognised there was a part of me saying 'I don't deserve to park in the nice car park' and I can hear myself slip into child victim mode as I write this! Then I almost justified this by telling myself 'I can't afford to park in the nice car park' (hence my internal bully creeping in!).

So, I recognised I had a choice! I asked myself whether I could afford to park in the nice car park nearer to where I was meeting my friend. The answer was yes! I asked myself whether I would feel better by listening to my beliefs and parking in the nice car park, and of course the answer was also yes. So I parked in the nice car park and I felt great!

Stopping to think instead of being on automatic pilot made an incredible difference to my awareness. Ironically, the difference in price between the two car parks was 20p!

CHAPTER 5

Managing Your Expectations

I often come across people who have unrealistic expectations of themselves and others. As a result they are constantly striving to be better and rarely feeling good enough.

Having expectations that are too high may cause you to dismiss the good in yourself and others, and only focus on the bad.

One of my clients was new to stand-up comedy and, in the session after his second gig, he voiced how it hadn't been as good as he expected it to be, so he felt disappointed. In exploring his expectations, he thought it would be a brilliant gig and expected to be signing autographs afterwards. These expectations were unrealistic and as a result he had set himself up to feel like a failure. In further exploration, we were able to analyse his gig realistically, so he could appreciate what he had done really well such as interacting with the audience, trying out new material and being spontaneous.

I encourage you to think about your expectations of yourself? Do you often find yourself feeling not good enough and overwhelmed because you didn't achieve everything you wanted to get done in a day? Do you then criticise yourself about all the things you didn't manage to achieve?

If so, I can relate to this. I had a deep-rooted belief that I wasn't good enough, so I would unconsciously set out a **self-fulfilling** prophecy that would confirm this belief every day!

How did I do this?

Most days I would make a list of things I wanted to do that day. My list used to be very unrealistic so as a result:

'I set myself out to fail before I had even started my day!'

At the end of the day, even though I had done loads, I would only focus on what I hadn't done and would give myself a hard time for it! By giving myself a hard time I would end up feeling not good enough - hence a self-fulfilling prophecy!

If you can relate to this, then you have the choice to take a step back and look at your own expectations.

Here are some questions to help you understand your expectations:

Managing your expectations

How many things do you expect to achieve in a day?

Is this realistic given the time you have?

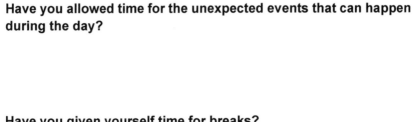

Have you allowed time for the unexpected events that can happen during the day?

Have you given yourself time for breaks?

If your best friend had this list of expectations, what would you think?

One way to manage your expectations is to make sure your list is realistic and achievable, giving you a fair chance of completing your actions. Imagine the feeling of satisfaction and achievement when you can tick them all off at the end of the day. I find that, because I don't put unrealistic expectations on myself, I usually end up doing more because I have taken the pressure off and I'm just enjoying the process. The good news is:

'Less is more!'

Managing your expectations starts with you being less hard on yourself, especially if you struggle with an underlying core belief of not feeling good enough.

I often see highly driven people who say "I've got to have it" or "I've got to do it now"...but they don't think about the consequences i.e. the effect on their health, relationships, family etc. You need to think about who is cracking the whip and why you're being so hard on yourself?

To be less hard on yourself you need to **manage your expectations** of yourself. Remember – less is more!

Managing your expectations of others

It is important that you manage your expectations of others, and don't expect others to be how you want them to be, as we are all responsible for ourselves.

'We choose how we want to be and it's important we allow others to do the same.'

For example, when I think of my expectations I would love to hear my mum tell me that she loves me. The difference now is I don't expect her to say it. I know this is something she is not comfortable doing and I accept this. I don't expect her to say it to me and as a result I don't get left feeling disappointed. I have managed my own expectations. I know the reality is that, just because she doesn't say it, that doesn't mean she doesn't love me. I know she does and she shows me this in many other ways.

Different Perspectives

People have many different perspectives on life. If someone is used to being criticised then it's likely they will be critical of you. This can be before you have even done anything. Sometimes people say things and are completely unaware of how they might affect you. You have the option to communicate this to them in a nice way, to help make them aware of how their words can sometimes come across, and to let them know how they can verbally support you, especially if their intent is to help you.

For example, a friend of mine said to me before a gig: "You better be good!". I automatically felt pressured. I explored her statement and accepted that I would be the best I could be, and that is enough. Luckily I had others tell me they couldn't wait to see me perform which encouraged me and spurred me on, and fits in with my morals and values of letting ourselves go and just having a good time. I spoke to my friend about her statement and she was horrified to hear how it initially affected me, when she meant it as a joke.

What other people think

As mentioned, people come from many different perspectives. Some people come from a place of jealousy and can tell you things to bring you down. Other people approach life from their own limitations, and without knowing will limit you with their thoughts and actions. Others may come from a place of conditioning and learned behaviour and believe you are only as good as what someone else tells you.

Many people from past generations were taught that self-praise was bragging and that it was wrong. For me it's all about balance. I spent so many years being put down and continuing to do it to myself that it is very important I recognise when I'm actually doing well.

To give you an example, comedy can be very subjective. What one person finds funny another doesn't, so it is impossible to please everyone. I don't expect everyone to like my humour. All I can do is my best – some jokes will work, some won't. When we look at this with perspective and understanding we see people have a right to choose what is funny. So who am I to change that! Instead, I choose to focus on the people who do enjoy my sense of humour.

It really doesn't matter what others think of you.

Trying to please everyone is a regular piece of conditioning that I come across constantly with my clients. This type of thinking and conditioning only leads to more low self-worth. How tiring it can be to feel like you have to please everyone. It is impossible to please everyone so trying to do so can be very frustrating.

'It doesn't matter what other people think of you, it's what you think of you.'

CHAPTER 6

Making Assumptions

The process of making assumptions is also known as N.A.T.S.[6] which stands for Negative Automatic Thoughts. This is when you assume something before you know the facts.

It is important to be aware of other people's assumptions.

> For example, I wanted to join Equity so I spoke to a woman who owns a recording studio. She told me there was no point in applying as I would not get my Equity card because I needed to have done a whole list of things to be approved. Luckily for me, I ignored her assumptions. I rang up Equity and within 10 minutes I got my Equity card. The woman had not taken the time to find out the facts about my experiences before assuming I would not get one. If I had been easily lead, as I have been in the past, I would have believed this woman's assumptions and not have bothered to apply to Equity for fear of rejection.

---

6. Aaron T. Beck/Albert Ellis 'Negative automatic thoughts'

Another example of this was when I took my car to the garage to get the clutch fixed. After I'd paid, I drove off, but the clutch still wasn't working properly. I had to drive my car back to the garage at 10 miles an hour on a busy street. I worked hard to maintain my state of mind and drive as near to the side of the road as possible. I put on my hazard lights so people would know I was having a problem with my car and could drive past me. My main fear was not making it! I had reassured myself that, since I was near a garage, they would have a tow truck to come and get me or a bunch of blokes to come and push my car!

When I told my story to a friend later, she said to me: "You must have been so embarrassed!". Actually I was just relieved to get the car back and I hadn't even thought about embarrassment until she mentioned it. Should I have been embarrassed? Would the feeling of being embarrassed have helped me? Would the drivers in the other cars have cared if I was embarrassed or not? Obviously not.

You can see from these examples how people can project their assumptions onto you. Therefore, before you take on other people's perceptions and assumptions, always stop and think:

'What is best for you?'

I encourage you not to assume things, especially when you don't know the facts, and not to take on the assumptions of others if they are not based on hard evidence. Find out things for yourself. Make your own decisions and enjoy taking full responsibility for the decisions you make.

CHAPTER 7

Depression

If someone constantly keeps putting unrealistic expectations onto themselves, this can lead to them feeling stressed, overwhelmed and can ultimately lead to depression.

There are many reasons why people get depressed, and it can happen to anyone.

In my experience of seeing clients, it's usually a mix of different things that, when combined, are just too overwhelming for a person to cope with.

Depression is labelled in various ways. Years ago, when someone suffered with depression, they were described as 'suffering with their nerves'. Often, these people weren't given the support needed to find out why they were depressed, or given any help to cope.

It can be difficult to recognise when you or someone you know has depression as it is not always obvious to see.

But how do you know when you or someone else is going through depression?

I remember discussing depression with someone. I was explaining that unless you have been through it, it is hard to understand. She agreed and said: "I've never gone through depression". She then said:

"I remember at one point in my life I felt like I couldn't cope. I was in bed for a week and had a black cloud hanging over me – but I've never been through depression."

You can see the irony in this statement. We all have good and bad days, but the downward spiral of depression happens when you live in the bad days and a black cloud creeps over you and stays there.

Depression can become so overwhelming that it can lead to suicidal thoughts like, 'What's the point?'.

If a person also has deep-rooted beliefs of low self-worth they might continue these negative thoughts with 'I'm going to fail anyway'. It's easy to see why, over time, a person can truly believe that the world would be a better place without them.

> Before I did therapy and trained to be a counsellor, I'm ashamed to say that I thought suicide was a selfish thing. From what I now know, and from dealing with my own depression I most certainly do not believe this anymore. I can see how someone can get so down that they see suicide as an option. It is so important that we become open to understanding depression.

When clients come to me they are usually in a very dark place. The negative thoughts have overwhelmed them and they are struggling to cope. Often, when this is the case, they are so hard on themselves that it's no wonder they are trapped in that cycle. I come across this on a regular basis where people are just too hard on themselves.

When people don't understand depression, and come across someone with depression, they can say things like 'snap out of it' or 'get a grip', but this is not helpful.

'If they could 'snap out of it', they would!'

For most people, when they are depressed they cannot think clearly and have irrational thoughts. Things feel more personal, they feel alone, confused and scared. This is where seeing a professional counsellor can help.

If you are reading this and know someone with depression, there are things you can do! Show them you care and be understanding. Ask them if there is anything you can do to help. Sometimes just being there is enough. Offer a listening ear, but listen without giving advice, as true listening allows the person to offload their thoughts and not feel judged.

Symptoms of Depression[7]

Although depression can sometimes be hard to physically see, it can have strong physical symptoms for the person suffering.

My physical symptoms of depression started as panic attacks, and I thought I was dying from a heart attack. Unless you have experienced one of these it is impossible to understand how horrendous a panic attack can be. I joke about this in comedy when I say:

"A panic attack is like an orgasm - you'll know when you've had one."

Another symptom I experienced, and still do to a lesser extent, is sore eyes, but the most severe symptom I experienced was the feeling of a massive weight on my head. It felt so physical that I was convinced I had a tumour. It took months for my counsellor to convince me that the weight on my head was suppressed emotions. It was so physically strong that I didn't believe her. I finally believed it was suppressed emotions because the only way I felt better was to cry or to get angry.

In dealing with clients, I have seen for myself how deep-rooted emotions can form into physical symptoms. There can be a lot of truth in the expression:

'Depression is merely anger without the enthusiasm.'

The triggers of depression can vary.

For me, long mirrors would trigger the memory of me being ridiculed in front of the mirror at home. I can now understand why going clothes shopping was very difficult for me.

---

7. www.rethink.org/diagnosis-treatment/conditions/depression

For other people, depression can be triggered from a one-off event, perhaps a trauma, bereavement or an abusive situation.

'Usually depression is a result of some form of loss.'

This could be a loss of youth, looks, career, relationships, family or something that the person would have wanted in the past but could not have.

Depression and anxiety can lead to behaviours like obsessive compulsive disorder, over-eating, panic attacks, addictions, fears and phobias.

How depression affects your thinking?

As mentioned, depression can cause irrational thoughts. Ever heard of the expression 'I can't see the wood for the trees'? This is when a person is so focused on a problem and are so consumed with bad feelings and thoughts, they can't see the solution.

Here are some examples of irrational thinking to help you tell if you are thinking clearly or not:

• **Fortune Telling** – thoughts like 'I just know it's going to turn out bad.'

• **All or nothing**[8] – 'It's either going to be brilliant or complete rubbish.'

• **Discounting the positives** – 'I was just lucky.'

• **Jumping to conclusions** – 'I'm going to fail again.'

• **Blaming** – 'It's all my fault' or 'He made me feel this way.'

• **Mind reading** – 'I know she thinks I'm stupid.'

• **'Should' statements** – 'I should have done it differently' or 'If only.'

• **Catastrophising/Exaggerating** – 'It's going to be the end of the world.'

You can see how someone can feel completely worthless by having these kind of thoughts. These kind of thoughts may lead you to see a distorted self.

---

8. Aaron T. Beck 'All-or-nothing thinking'

The B Line

Here is The B Line sheet, a Behaviour Line sheet to highlight 'the distorted self' and 'the true self'.

In 'the distorted self', circle any words that relate to you. You can revisit this diagram in six months time to see if there have been any changes.

THE B LINE
The Behaviour Line
THE DISTORTED SELF

These reflect behaviours as a result of seeing yourself through judgements, criticisms and unrealistic expectations.

Blame	Persecution
Anger	Hate
Procrastination	Criticising
Avoidance	Judgemental
Insecurity	Helplessness
Child victim mode	Debilitating
Perfectionism	Arrogance
Conditional	Greed
Low self-worth	Limiting beliefs
Unhealthy control	Manipulation
Defensive	Resentment
Negative thinking	Distorted thoughts
Unrealistic expectations	Assumptions
Generalising	Discounting compliments

In 'The B Line', 'the true self', circle any words that relate to you. You can revisit this diagram in six months time to see if there have been any changes.

THE B LINE
The Behaviour Line
THE TRUE SELF

This is when you see yourself with acceptance and love

Unconditional love	Acceptance
Self-responsibility	Congruence
Positive core beliefs	Autonomy
Equality	Openness
Rational thinking	Adult mode
Empathy	Patience
Being your own best friend	Accountability
Kindness	Gratitude
Peace	Happiness
Perspective	Nurturing
Self-respect	Respect for others
Empowerment	Support
Listening to gut instinct	Supportive beliefs
Positive thinking	Allowance
Acceptance of vulnerability	Care

Depression can make you want to shut yourself away. This is not helpful as shutting yourself away can often make you feel even more alone. Hence another self-fulfilling prophecy. I believe some people suffer from depression but don't speak about it for fear they will be treated differently. Ironically, most people have been through some kind of depression in their life, they just didn't know it. I was one of those people. If people talk about it more, the fear and stigma of depression will hopefully go, and it may be accepted as part of coping with life.

> When I spoke to my family individually and explained about my depression, the knock on effect was amazing. Speaking to them, and acknowledging my depression meant I didn't put myself under any more pressure to be 'happy Sheila'. This was a massive relief. I accepted that my depression came from suppressed emotions and distorted thinking from the abuse and bullying I experienced in the past.

I can only speak from my own experiences but, if you can relate to this, then you'll be pleased to know suppressed emotions can be offloaded in a healthy way, and distorted thinking can be changed!

The good news is that, if you are feeling depressed or going through depression, it doesn't have to always be this way. I encourage you to find a qualified counsellor who can help you. This is what I did, and as a result I now feel privileged to able to help others in the same way as a qualified counsellor myself.

CHAPTER 8

The Fear Of Letting Go

Something I have noticed from my own therapy and from working with my clients is that often the fear of offloading emotions is greater than the emotion itself.

For example, often in therapy a client will be afraid to get angry. They will say things like, "I don't do anger". It's important to realise that anger is a natural emotion, often triggered when something doesn't feel right. In fact, anger can be a great emotion when used in a healthy way.

Unfortunately, some people may have experienced anger in a very negative way. They may have seen or experienced physical violence when the anger was out of control. It is only natural then that there will be a fear around letting it go. They can be afraid that if they get angry they will absolutely lose it. In my experience and from my experiences of working with people:

'Holding down the anger takes more energy than actually letting it go.'

Often, when clients allow themselves to let go of their anger they can be amazed at how the fear of it was bigger than the anger itself.

The same applies to sadness. People can feel like they have to hold the grief in, especially if they have been conditioned to think this way. They may have been told things like, "Be strong!", "You are doing so well in the way you are holding it together". People mean well, but it takes more energy to hold in that natural emotion than to let it go. You are only human. As one of my clients said as a result of listening to her own needs:

"It's ok to let go."

I remember in my own therapy, my counsellor did an empty chair technique. She got me to imagine my brother was sitting in a chair so I could voice my sadness and anger towards him. I was so worried about being judged that I couldn't do it. I was afraid she would think I was stupid. As a result I continued to suppress the sadness and anger.

I also had a fear about being loved. I had felt rejected so many times that I was afraid to let go. I was afraid that if I did something she didn't like that I would be rejected again. Over time I built trust in my counsellor and learned she wasn't going to reject me if I did something wrong.

As my confidence has increased, I now realise that what other people think isn't important, as we all have our own issues. So, during my counselling training I allowed myself to let go of my anger and do the empty chair technique. Instantly, I felt relieved!

I now do this technique often in my own therapy and find it very powerful. If you like the sound of this technique, I would recommend you try this with a qualified counsellor.

CHAPTER 9

Offloading Emotions

It is normal for people to sometimes get frustrated, angry, anxious or sad as these are all natural human emotions. You may have heard of the expressions 'chin up', 'be strong' etc. which are all part of 'conditioning' as discussed in Chapter 3.

There may be times that you don't realise how angry you are until it is too late. It is important that you don't suppress your emotions but learn how to offload them safely so they don't build up over time.

I encourage you to offload your emotions and there are many safe ways to do this.

For some people, **playing a sport** like squash can help.

Other people like to **keep a journal** as **writing your thoughts down** can help. Try not to analyse or judge your writing and don't try to limit your words - just go for it!

For others, **talking to a friend** can help share a problem. Someone who will listen to you without judging you, and not tell you what to do.

Listening to music or watching a film can help you when feeling sad, to connect with your sadness and offload it. Alanis Morrissette's sad songs do it for me every time! Generally **having a good cry** helps. Some of my clients find that 'Fix you' by Coldplay is a great tear jerker. Some watch the Titanic movie. Do whatever helps you to connect with the sadness and offload it so you are not building it up inside.

Other people find that **martial arts, a brisk walk, running, artistic creative activities, writing poetry** or **writing songs** can be great way to offload frustration too.

Finally, an **anger cushion** comes highly recommended! This is great to use if you are feeling angry or frustrated and you want to take it out in a healthy way.

> I have supervision as part of my counselling work. I remember in one session, my supervisor highlighted how hard I was being on myself. I felt incredibly angry as I knew the past bullying was holding me back, and I was totally ignoring all the good stuff I had achieved. When I got home, I got my anger cushion (which is a big part of my sofa) and battered the life out it! I was exhausted afterwards, but it stopped me giving myself a hard time and after having offloaded I felt great!

In my experience:

'You have your own solutions – sometimes you just need help to let your own answers shine through.'

I now recognise that, in the past, I used poetry to offload my emotions. Some of these poems are very dark. I used to be shocked by how I felt, however now I'm not anymore as I understand where it all came from. I then naturally progressed into writing songs as a way to offload my emotions.

I plan to publish and share these poems and songs in the hope they may bring reassurance to others who have felt or are feeling the same way, to help people recognise they are not alone.

Nowadays, when I get a cloud of depression come over me I find it best to write down my thoughts. If I am working, or not in a position to do self-counselling, I acknowledge the symptoms and make a time slot in my day to work on this. I don't always know what the trigger is, but I know the worst thing I can do is just ignore it and expect it to go away. I know it's another bit of suppressed emotion that needs to come out.

Whatever you decide it is important to set a time limit.

When I feel a weight on my head, I know it's suppressed emotions so I give my-self 15 to 30 minutes of listening to sad music to connect with the sadness, or, if I'm feeling angry, I get angry with the anger cushion on my sofa!

My process of self-counselling starts by me writing things down without any judgements or expectations. Below are the words I wrote when the black cloud was over me and I was feeling worthless. I need to pre-warn you that there is bad language in this piece, so you have the choice if you want to read it or not. I have copied it down word for word to be authentic, and to show you the kind of thoughts that people can have when feeling depressed.

It's a beautiful day outside yet inside I feel I could die. The pain inside me feels so intense. It stops me from enjoying myself. It stops me from feeling good and it stops me from being me. I'm feeling sick of it. So fucking sick of it. So fucking sick of having an underlying feeling of pure raw pain. If this pain could speak it would say, "Why?" I'm feeling so isolated. Feeling of no self-worth. Like I don't deserve anything good to happen to me. Who the fuck is saying this? I feel like I don't have the energy to fight it. I feel worn down. I feel like giving up. I hate connecting to this pain. It's so raw. Pains on my chest, sore throat. I feel so lucky that this emotional shit hasn't manifested itself into a serious illness. Again relief when I cry.

Feels like this pain has been there for a long time and it's now coming to the surface. I don't know how to overcome it.

It's so fucking consuming, overwhelming. I can't think straight when I feel it and it feels like it takes over me when I do give into it. When I feel like this I want to sleep and never wake up again. WHY? Why did you make me feel like shit? Why did you treat me so bad? I just wanted to be loved. I just wanted to be loved. This pain is from my inner child not from the adult me. Inner child needs comfort. Reassurance that people won't let her down. So much change is happening. Inner child is scared. Scared of the consequences. Scared of letting go. Scared of shining for fear of being beat up, shamed, ridiculed. Ahh Sheila it's ok. No-one can harm you now. It's ok to come out. I feel like part of me is locked away in my bedroom and afraid to come out. It's a nasty world out there. I'll get hurt. Oh God I need you. I need you so much. Give my inner child the courage to come out. To believe everything will be ok. That people are not out to get me. That I can be brilliant, fabulous and gorgeous. That I deserve to be loved. That I deserve great things to happen to me. I want to feel truly loved.

Most of the time when I write stuff down I can spot where the trigger came from. Usually it's some situation or person that reminded me of the past. After I have a good cry or get angry I then pull myself out of it. I make a conscious decision that I am not going to let these negative thoughts and feelings get the better of me for the rest of the day. So I think about what I love and do something different with my body to shake myself out of child victim state into adult mode. I do this by going for a walk or dancing to the 'Macarena'!

This is about whatever works for you! Ask yourself the following question:

How can I offload my emotions without harming myself or anyone else?

The important thing is to make time to get these emotions out so they don't keep holding you back!

Losing the plot!

I can relate to what happens when you don't offload emotions.

When I was 12 years old, my friend and I managed to get into my primary school when it was closed, just for a bit of fun. At first it was exciting, but as I walked into one of the classrooms, I remembered the times I felt belittled there. I remembered being told to walk up in front of the class and write on the board that I was lazy. Everyone was laughing at me. I remembered feeling ridiculed. Then I remembered all the times I felt ridiculed at home by my brothers and ignored by my parents and I lost the plot!

I saw red, started throwing things around and damaged photographs and books. In fact I lost the plot so much that I can't remember all the things I did. I was out of control. Eventually I calmed down and spent the next four days in sheer panic, terrified and confused about what I had done and what was going to happen next. The police were called in, and I was very lucky I didn't end up with a criminal record. As a result I was banned from ever seeing my best friend again. My mother was shocked with my behaviour.

Now, as an adult, I understand why I did it. Of course I wish I hadn't and I am still deeply sorry to the people I affected. The shame in this story is, it was a cry for help. My parents never took the time to understand why I did it. There was only so much bullying I could take before I was going to flip!

It is very dangerous to build up your anger and frustration to a point that it is out of control. As in my example above, it can lead to regretting things that were not intended. As an adult you have the choice to take responsibility for yourself by doing activities that help you to offload the frustrations in your life in a healthy way.

If you don't feel able to offload your emotions, then I encourage you to find a qualified counsellor or other professional who can help you with this.

CHAPTER 10

The Fear Of Failure

A lot of people have an underlying fear of failure, but what is failure? It can make you feel not good enough – but by whose standards? The truth is there is no such thing as failure. You need to fail to learn. So failure is actually learning.

You and I make mistakes because we are human and not robots.

However, if you are a person that thinks 'If I fail no-one will like me, or even love me', then you may go out of your way to be a perfectionist. By trying so hard and ignoring that you are only human, you may set yourself up to fail - again another self-fulfilling prophecy. If you can relate to this then I encourage you to be less hard on yourself. It's ok to be a high achiever, as long as you are doing it for the right reasons.

'In my experience of being counselled and being a counsellor, I believe a lot of what we do is led by the need to be loved.'

If the people around you really love you then they won't judge you when you do something wrong. They will want what is best for you and will encourage you to try again. If they do judge you, then it really is their problem, as you have a right to learn and to make mistakes without being judged. The most important thing about failure is how you see it. I encourage you to:

'Allow yourself to fail – it's very liberating.'

By facing the fear of failure, you allow yourself to be human, and you set yourself free. It's one of the kindest gifts you can give yourself.

CHAPTER 11

Understanding
Deep-rooted Emotions

Anger, resentment, guilt and blame.

Some of the main emotions I had to offload and learn to understand were anger and resentment. I was angry at my parents for not emotionally supporting me when I was younger.

Through therapy, I began to realise that my parents didn't intentionally want to make me feel rubbish. I learned to accept that, even though their behaviour gave me the impression I was not loved, that I really was loved.

I remember a friend saying to me that if they had a younger sister, they would protect her and look out for her. I felt very sad by this, as my experience was nothing like that and I realised I craved that.

'I went through a process of grieving
for the childhood I never had.'

I was also angry at myself because I continued to bully myself for years and years. After going through therapy and offloading lots of sadness and anger this has made a huge difference in overcoming my self-limitations.

I also learned how to forgive my parents, my brothers and most of all to forgive myself. As part of my therapy, I spoke to my brothers who totally acknowledged that they mistreated me, and apologised. I am very lucky to have had this experience, as it can be very difficult when people don't own up to their behaviour.

My brothers have grown up to be respectful, caring men and I am very proud of them.

Therapy also helped me to understand that my parents were doing their best, that they did love me and that they meant well. They showed me their love in practical ways like putting food on the table, a roof over my head and helping me financially. They didn't know how to give emotional, unconditional love because it was never given to them. Parents learn from their parents.

'If they were not given support, encouragement and emotional love, how can they give it to anyone else?'

This inspired me to write a poem called 'How are we to know?'.

How are we to know?

When we are born we are born pure
To the mercy of our world
And depending on how we are conditioned
It can be beautiful or be blurred

Regardless of how our parents grew up
We put them on a pedestal
We hang on to their every word
Believing that they mean well

But what if they were suppressed
By judgements, expectations and fear
Then pass these on unbeknown to them
And we become bitter throughout the years

And because we all need to be loved
We may not feel right to challenge them
Then we choose to have children
And the cycle starts all over again

But there is light for we can change
And we don't have to keep doing the same
We can build our awareness, take responsibility for ourselves
And let go of this limiting pain

Our lives are how we want to be
We don't have to just go with the flow
We have got choices of which path to take
And we have a right to say no

We all deserve self-respect
To be valued in what we do
To not be judged, allowed to grow
And this starts with how you feel about you

So regardless of who brought you up
Regardless of what was right or wrong
As adults we can take responsibility for ourselves
And choose how we want to live on

So be who you want to be
Don't let fear hold you back
Allow your inner light to shine through
And it will guide you through the black

Surround yourself with people who unconditionally love you
Environments that help you to grow
And if self-blame ever creeps in, just think
How were we to know?

Think about how you feel about the people who influenced you in relation to this poem. Write your own reflections here.

CHAPTER 12

Acceptance

As I read the previous poem, I am overwhelmed at how far I have come. I used to have the weight on my head and sore eyes every day. Now I hardly get it at all, and when I do it's ok – I know how to deal with it and I accept where these symptoms come from.

This is where I needed to learn acceptance. It reminds me of the quote:

'Accept the things I cannot change.'

This quote may help you to move on from the past, to acknowledge it and learn to accept it. Accepting it means you gain back control of your life. It means you decide that instead of fighting it, you accept it, learn from it and consciously decide to not live there anymore. Acceptance of myself means I accept I cannot change the past but I can learn from it. To be honest, I don't want to get rid of the past as that has made me who I am today. As a result of my experience, when I'm counselling clients I can totally empathise with them when they offload similar experiences.

I accept that, because of the past and because I am only human I will have bad days, and that's ok. Again I quote one of my clients:

"It's ok not to be ok."

Ask yourself:

> **How can I be more accepting of myself?**
>
>
>
>
> **What would it feel like to say to myself, 'It's ok not to be ok'?**

I see so many times on social media how some people put down what they want you to see. It's another form of 'keeping up with the Joneses'.

For example, I was at a wedding and there were two women sitting at a table looking bored and miserable. This continued for a while until one woman said: "Let's put a photo on Facebook". The woman then turned her camera to face them both and by some miracle their faces lit up as if they were having a great time. One of the women looked at the picture and said: "No, not happy enough, let's take it again.", so they did, and this time with even brighter glowing smiles! Then they went back to being bored and miserable.

Out of curiosity, I had a look at what they wrote beside their picture and it said: 'Having a great time, wish you were here.'!

Some people feel they have to be happy 24 hours a day, 7 days a week, as if it's a competition to prove that they are the happiest people on earth.

The problem is, when you come from a place of unhealthy competitiveness and desire to be better than others, there are no winners. I believe:

'It's actually harder to pretend you are happy when you are not.'

The good news is, that when you accept you are only human and entitled to have bad days, you may laugh about it and be less hard on yourself. When you come from a place of acceptance you see each other as equal, the world as fair game and you are able to be happy for others even when you are not happy within yourself. Try to accept the bad days and to be less hard on yourself.

Patience

I would say another part of acceptance is patience. How patient are you? It reminds me of the saying 'Good things come to those who wait'. If you rush into things, you may self-sabotage your good work. You may be so eager to please and get something done that you may end up unhappy with the results. If patience is something that you struggle with, start by first acknowledging it. Become aware of the impact impatience has on you and the people around you. Explore new ways of how you can be more patient. Sometimes forcing things only makes it worse. I encourage you to accept the things that are out of your control, be kind to yourself and see time as your friend.

CHAPTER 13

Forgiveness

Forgiveness was definitely one of the biggest obstacles I had to overcome. In my experience:

'When you hold on to bitterness and resentment, the person you are hurting the most is you.'

Forgiveness for me came after I understood why my parents and brothers behaved in the way they did.

As previously mentioned, as part of my therapy I talked to my brothers about how they had treated me, and the impact of their behaviour - they were horrified.

In my experience of working with clients, most bullies are not aware of how they are coming across. This doesn't make it right, but it may help you to forgive and understand it more. Sometimes they are bullying because of frustration and anger within their own lives.

When you look at bullying from a different perspective, it allows you to see that a lot of times it might not be personal. When you look at it from a place of understanding, it may allow you to accept it and to forgive.

As part of the research for this book I spoke to my brothers to gain an even deeper understanding of where they were coming from and to hear what it was like from their perspective. I learned they didn't understand why they behaved in the way they did. I learned that they were bullied too.

I now understand what they did. They didn't know how to support and love me. In speaking to one of my brothers he voiced how the notion of him seeing his sister as a friend didn't enter his mind. This did not come natural to them, which leads to the 'How are we to know?' poem, as my parents were not shown and allowed to be this way themselves as children.

I know my brothers still deeply regret how they treated me. However, now the best thing they can do for me is to forgive themselves.

How you forgive is an individual thing. What has helped me and some of my clients is writing a letter to the people who have hurt you the most. It's up to you if you want to send it or not, as it can just be used as an exercise to help you offload suppressed emotions. Regardless of whether they are dead or alive, still in contact with you or not, this exercise can be a vital part of the healing process to let the past go.

I have totally forgiven my brothers and my parents for they did not know what they were doing.

As part of this forgiveness and therapeutic process, I have come to understand why I continued to treat myself in a bad way. A lot of it was learned behaviour, as by my brothers bullying me I learned how to continue to bully myself. A lot of it was self-blame as I continued to carry the blame for what happened. I was a victim and a bully at the same time.

Now, because I understand it, I can forgive myself. I do still have good days and bad, but the difference is I don't give myself a hard time over it – I accept I am only a human just doing my best, and that is good enough.

We've all made mistakes in the past. A lot of the time people didn't know they had choices and did the best they knew at the time.

I encourage you to forgive. Forgive others but most of all forgive yourself.

'By forgiving I set myself free.'

CHAPTER 14

Coping Mechanisms

To find the best coping mechanisms for you, it is important to become aware of what coping mechanisms you have learned in the past.

For example, the first thing of value I owned as a child was my bike, but my brothers would trash this bike whenever they could. I remember being about 10 years old and seeing the front wheel of my bike at a 90 degree angle. They thought this was hilarious. I was crying my eyes out.

I remember getting a picture from my Aunt. I remember the feeling of actually owning something. It felt great, yet as I held it, I wanted to smash it. For those few minutes I felt in control. I wanted to do something with it before that bit of control was taken away from me. I spent many years not understanding why I wanted to smash that picture, but I do understand it now!

As a result of things being taken away from me, I felt like I didn't deserve to own anything. As a result of my experience, I learned not to value anything as I believed it would be damaged or taken away from me.

I am aware this was my coping mechanism as a child.

'I learned not value things so when they were taken away it wouldn't hurt so much.'

As the years went by I became aware that I would deliberately mistreat things. This is not a good coping mechanism as an adult, as it is important that I do value things and believe I deserve to have valuable things! Can you see how understanding the past is vital to spot self-sabotaging habits?

Coping Mechanisms

What coping mechanisms did you learn in the past?

Are there any coping mechanisms you used in the past that might be having a negative impact on who you are now?

If so, are there any other coping mechanisms you can use instead?

If you feel unable to answer these questions then I would highly recommend you work with a qualified counsellor to find out what coping mechanisms you developed in the past. It may help you to understand why you developed them and how they might be impacting on you now.

Emotional Eating

Another negative coping mechanism I used as a child was emotional eating. Food was a great source of comfort to me. At that time, I felt it gave me pleasure without criticising me and judging me. I used to eat in secret, and it instantly made me feel good. As a child I wasn't aware of the implications of eating too much.

'Food for me at that time replaced love.'

It took me a long time to accept that bingeing and stuffing my face was doing me no favours. I really didn't want to let this coping mechanism go, however I would feel rubbish after I had eaten too much. Through counselling, I became aware of how this coping mechanism also became a punishment. I would stuff my face because deep down I didn't believe I deserved to look and feel good. It was when I forgave myself and stopped carrying the self-blame that I was able to treat my body with respect. Now, as an adult, I meet my needs of love in other ways. I taught myself how to see food in a healthy way and allowed myself to look and feel good. I still have days where I stuff my face but the difference is, I accept that I am only human and don't give myself a hard time about it.

As an adult I am constantly learning new coping mechanisms. Some of the thoughts that really help me are:

'See past the event.'

I use this when I get nervous before some gigs, especially when I'm performing my own comedy shows as I include a lot of new material for the first time. What helps me to put this show into perspective is to see past the event. If the show is on a Friday, then I think about what I'll be doing on the Saturday.

Sometimes, when you get nervous about an upcoming event, the more you focus on it the bigger it may seem. This can become overwhelming, as if your whole world is only about this event. This is not reality. Life goes on regardless of how the event goes.

'What's the worst that can happen?'

This was a great coping mechanism for me when I first moved to the UK. If the worst happened I could just move back to Ireland, but by trying it in the first place meant I would live with no regrets about not knowing.

I also use this coping mechanism when it comes to my new shows. The worst that can happen is no-one laughs and they don't like my material. As a comedienne I accept that I won't always have great gigs.

'I give myself permission to fail.'

How else can I learn? So, if the worst happens, at least I can learn from it!

You can find more coping mechanisms later on in the 'Managing your mind' section in chapter 16 of this book.

It's important to note that some people cope by simply blocking out old memories. This works for some people and they live normal happy lives, but not for others.

If it doesn't work for you, it may continue to hold you back until you deal with it. This may lead to self-sabotaging behaviour until you deal with the deep-rooted problem. I have definitely been one of those people.

In writing this book, I noticed that when I felt depressed and did some self counselling on myself, my sadness felt very deep and very young. I had a gut instinct there was more that needed to come out. This confirms my belief that:

'The answers are within you.'

I couldn't remember, so I spoke to my family who confirmed that I had blocked out more of what had happened to me. So, for me, the depression was a coping mechanism, and a sign that something was still wrong and needed to be dealt with. I believe this came out later when I was ready to deal with it, and could let the self-blame go.

CHAPTER 15

State Of Mind

I mentioned 'inner child' earlier in the book. Every adult has experienced being a child, and sometimes an adult can unconsciously act like that child when they are an adult. This can be described as them being in a child state of mind. Other states of mind include adult and parent state of mind. Adult state of mind is when you are acting like an adult and living in the present. Parent state of mind is when you may take on the behaviours of your parents. There are deeper levels to this but for this book I focus on child, adult and parent state of mind to highlight the different behaviours. This is linked to Transaction Analysis Therapy originally defined by Eric Berne. If you want to read more about this then I would recommend reading 'TA Today' by Ian Stewart and Vann Joines.

For now let's look at the 'child state', as this may help you to learn from your past.

As a child, most of the time I saw the world as confusing. I felt unloved and thought everyone was out to get me. This was based on my experiences. This relates to me being in a 'victim child state of mind'. In victim mentality I had thoughts like 'why is this happening to me?' and 'what did I do wrong?', as well as an all over feeling of worthlessness. At that time I was a victim, so it would makes sense I felt that way.

However, there is also the 'free child', the child who regardless of what was going on still managed to have fun and could just let go.

Now as an adult, being in a victim child state of mind does not do me any good.

Victim state of mind comes from a place of helplessness.

'When you are in victim mode, you give your own personal power away and you blame everyone else for what happens.'

In this state of mind, you take no responsibility for yourself.

As an adult I am no longer a victim. However, when triggers or situations remind me of the past I can unconsciously slip into a victim child state of mind.

Here is an example of this in recent events:

There was work being done on the kitchen, with lots of drilling going on, which was very loud and frustrating. At the same time, the apartment below me was also having work done, so it felt like it was coming from all angles. I started to feel anxious, frustrated and very much in a victim state of mind. I started thinking 'why is this happening to me?', and it felt personal! (Can you see the distorted thinking here and the victim mentality!)

I thought about how I felt at that moment, and I felt like I did when I was eight years old. At the age of eight, I felt trapped as I was getting bullied from all angles – hence the frustration.

I realised I wasn't being bullied now, so I just acknowledged the sadness it reminded me of, and I allowed myself to cry. Ironically it was like reverse psychology as because I allowed myself to cry, I only cried for about 3 minutes!

I decided I didn't have to stay in and listen to this, so I thought about my options which was me taking responsibility for myself. I decided to take my work into the local park and do it there so I claimed back my own personal power.

I went from victim child state of mind to an adult state of mind.

As part of maintaining your state of mind and taking responsibility for yourself, it is important to accept that you get what you focus on. It's the same as if you wake up and think 'I'm going to have a bad day today', which means you most likely will, as that is what you are focusing on!

You can choose what you focus on and you can choose your state of mind.

It's easier to maintain your state of mind when you are in the right place. It rarely works if you have a black cloud of depression hanging over you. If the underlying emotions of sadness, anger or frustration are too strong, then more professional help is needed for you to offload these emotions in a healthy way. The right kind of professional assistance can help you to understand the underlying issues so you can maintain a healthy state of mind.

When you are aware, and have dealt with deep-rooted issues, then maintaining your state becomes easier – especially the more you do it!

Adult state of mind is the best place to be. You are in adult state of mind when you are in the present. You know you are in adult state when you are thinking clearly, logically and rationally. In adult state you look at things objectively and don't take them personally.

For me, as an adult it is important that I take responsibility for how I think and feel. I'm very aware that I get what I focus on. So if I stay in victim mode[9] and believe that everyone is out to get me, it means I'm still living my life through my experiences of the past. I'm living my life in a victim child state of mind which is not going to do me any good!

Seeing the child in me as a damaged victimised child led to me bullying myself. I choose to stop suppressing and blaming myself for the things that happened in the past.

'By allowing myself to connect with my inner free child, and meet my inner child's fun needs, I became whole and free.'

Through my awareness and new experiences, I have challenged my thinking as a victim child and proved to myself that most people are great and not out to get me. I have connected with my own personal power, and now believe I am a valued member of society. As I result I feel more in control. This then puts me back into an adult state of mind.

9. Dr. Karpman 'karpmandramatriangle'

Being in a victim child state didn't just affect my behaviour, it also affected the behaviour of others around me.

> For example, when I go back to the house I grew up in, certain rooms can remind me of the past. Sometimes I would go back into a child victim state of mind and as a result I would behave like a child. Because of this psychological game I was playing, my mum would start to treat me like a child, criticising and telling me off. She was then in a critical parent state of mind. This created a pattern of negative behaviour.

I changed this by recognising my own part to play in this behaviour. I worked on keeping myself in adult mode. As a result, my mother started speaking to me as an adult as she moved into adult mode too!

People's behaviour can be fascinating. Often people mirror each other and they can also mirror each other's state of minds. Try the exercise below.

Take a step back and see if you can see when adults are in victim child mode, free child mode, critical parent mode or being in adult mode in the here and now. Write down your reflections here.

To manage your state you need to manage your mind!

CHAPTER 16

Managing Your Mind

Your mind is made up of thoughts. Some good and some bad. You have the power to control what you choose to focus on. When you fully accept that you choose your thoughts, then you claim back your own personal power.

Your thoughts come from your beliefs. Some of your beliefs come from learned behaviour, some come from conditioning, and some come from distorted connections from childhood. Examples of distorted connections are in the 'My story from a child's point of view' section at the start of the book, where I internalised things incorrectly as a result of my experiences.

Another example of a distorted belief is someone who is very successful and wealthy, but they can't enjoy their wealth for fear they might lose it. You get what you focus on, so if that person is so focused on losing their wealth, it may become a self-fulfilling prophecy.

If you want to be the best you can be then you need to be aware of the impact that your negative thoughts are having on you, and how these negative thoughts and experiences might be limiting you and holding you back from your potential.

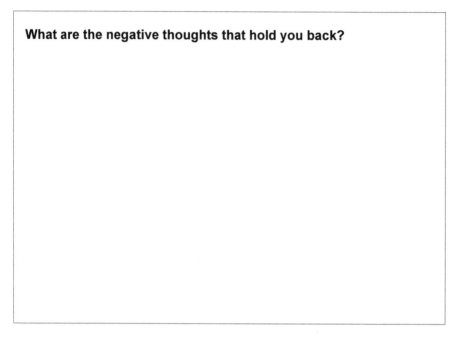

What are the negative thoughts that hold you back?

Ignoring negative thoughts doesn't make them go away, so I encourage you to write them down, so you can acknowledge them, and understand where they come from. You can build up your confidence, so when the negative thoughts come, you can challenge them so they don't keep holding you back.

The next exercise is a 'managing your thoughts' sheet. It is in three parts. The first part helps you to be aware of the impact that the negative thought has on you. The second part helps you to challenge it. The third part helps you to change it. This sheet takes time and highlights the impact of negative thinking.

If this is too much for you to do on your own, then I encourage you to do this with a qualified counsellor who will give you the unconditional, non-judgemental support you may need.

To help, I've included an example of a completed sheet from my past, based on how I was feeling about myself. I have filled this out to highlight my negative thought, and how it was impacting and limiting my life. I was going through depression when I answered these questions, so everything was dark and gloomy.

Example Sheet: (In three parts)

Managing your thoughts
Part 1 - What is my negative thought?

I'm not good enough

What does this thought say about me? *I'm not good at anything*

What does it say I can't do? *Anything*

What does this mean about me? *I've no talents and no abilities*

My life? *I will never feel satisfied and happy*

My future? *It makes me think 'What's the point' as I will only fail*

What does this mean about what other people might think or feel about me? *They may think I'm a fraud and really see that I am not good enough*

Is there a trigger or a certain time when I feel this way? *When I'm around judgemental people, when I feel under pressure*

What am I afraid might happen? *I will look and feel bad*

What facts (not opinions) suggest this is true? *I lack consistency*

What is the worst thing that could happen if this is true? *It confirms what I already believe*

What can I do if this does happen? *I can do something about it. Find the right support for me so I don't keep feeling this way*

Do I have any images or memories that are linked with this thought? *Yes as a child*

Does it remind me of another situation in my life? *My childhood, constant line of failed relationships*

How is this thought limiting my life? *Makes me feel worthless*

Managing your thoughts
Part 2 - Challenging the thought

Is there any factual evidence to suggest this thought is not 100% true? *I have achieved some things*

Have I had any experiences that show that this thought is not completely true all of the time? *Yes*

Am I jumping to conclusions that are not completely justified by the evidence? *I could be*

Am I blaming myself for something over which I do not have complete control? *I suppose, as a child I was limited in what I could achieve*

Do I have any unrealistic expectations with this thought? *Yes because I'm judging myself on my limited experiences*

If my best friend or someone who loves me knew I was thinking this thought, what would they say to me? *I'm being too hard on myself*

What evidence would they point out to me that would suggest that my thought is not 100% true? *They would tell me all the things I have achieved*

Are there any strengths or positives in me that I am ignoring? *I do have abilities to do great things, I just need to give myself a chance*

Five years from now, if I look back on this situation, will I look at it differently? *I certainly hope so. I don't want to feel worthless anymore*

Managing your thoughts
Part 3 - Perspective and Positivity

If my best friend or someone I loved had this thought, what would I tell them? *I'd say they were being unfair to themselves*

How would I suggest that they change this thought to sound more positive? *I'd encourage them to tell themselves they are good enough*

When I am not feeling this way, do I think about this type of situation any differently? How? *Yes I just get on and enjoy things without this internal critic holding me back*

What did I think that helped me feel better? *Why not try new things and allow myself to get good at them*

What would be an alternative way of thinking that encourages, inspires and supports me? *I'm just as good as anyone else*

Perspective and Positive thought

<u>I am good enough and deserve
to feel good enough</u>

It is hard for me to read what I wrote in part 1 as I feel so differently now.

Now it's your turn. I encourage you to write down the most limiting thought you have and to challenge it.

Managing your thoughts
Part 1 - What is my negative thought?

....

What does this thought say about me?

What does it say I can't do?

What does this mean about me?

My life?

My future?

What does this mean about what other people might think or feel about me?

Is there a trigger or a certain time when I feel this way?

If so what am I afraid might happen?

What facts (not opinions) suggest this is true?

What is the worst thing that could happen if this is true?

What can I do if this does happen?

Do I have any images or memories that are linked with this thought?

Does it remind me of another situation in my life?

How is this thought limiting my life?

Managing your thoughts
Part 2 - Challenging the thought

Is there any factual evidence to suggest this thought is not 100% true?

Have I had any experiences that show that this thought is not completely true all of the time?

Am I jumping to conclusions that are not completely justified by the evidence?

Am I blaming myself for something over which I do not have complete control?

Do I have any unrealistic expectations with this thought?

If my best friend or someone who loves me knew I was thinking this thought, what would they say to me?

What evidence would they point out to me that would suggest that my thought is not 100% true?

Are there any strengths or positives in me that I am ignoring?

Five years from now, if I look back on this situation, will I look at it differently?

Managing your thoughts
Part 3 - Perspective and Positivity

If my best friend or someone I loved had this thought, what would I tell them?

How would I suggest that they change this thought to sound more positive?

When I am not feeling this way, do I think about this type of situation any differently? How? What did I think that helped me feel better?

What would be an alternative way of thinking that encourages, inspires and supports me?

Perspective and Positive thought

....

At the end of this process you will hopefully have some positive thoughts to tell yourself, to overcome the negative conditioning and to become your own best friend.

Nowadays, instead of a 'managing your thoughts' sheet I fill in a one page daily tracker that puts my negative thought into perspective. I purposely haven't used this in this book as the questions will hopefully uncover any deep-rooted negative beliefs that may have been holding you back.

When new positive thoughts emerge, these can be also called affirmations.

Affirmations[10]

Affirmations are statements that are helpful, encouraging and supportive. Affirmations are non-judgemental and allow you to self-support. I encourage you to think about what encouraging thoughts you need to hear right now, as it's important to acknowledge your current feelings. For example, it could be statements like, 'even though I am feeling anxious, everything will sort itself out', 'even though I feel lost, time is a great healer and I know in time I will feel better' or 'even though I feel uncertain, it's ok for me not to feel ok right now'. Think about what relates to you and what you feel you need to hear.

I encourage you to say these statements using an empowering voice and to say it like you mean it!

In my experience of counselling myself and others we need to constantly do and say things that make us feel good about ourselves to maintain consistency.

You can find different examples of affirmations on the internet to suit you.

Affirmations can be very powerful.

To manage my mind and my state I use affirmations as part of my morning routine to ensure I keep my negative beliefs from the past, in the past!

10. Dr. Mercola 'Emotional freedom technique'

CHAPTER 17

Relationships

Your experience of relationships in the past may have a big impact on your relationships now. I encourage you to explore these questions:

Exploring your relationships

What have your relationships been like in the past?

Have there been similar negative patterns of behaviour?

Do some of your relationships not work out?

Is there always someone else to blame?

Having been bullied for years, it was a behaviour I was used to, so unconsciously I would attract some guys who were bullies. Even though I didn't want this, it felt comfortable. I was also in victim mode, didn't want to take responsibility for my choices and wanted someone to save me so I didn't have to save myself. That way:

'When things went wrong I always had someone else to blame.'

There were always massive dramas in my past relationships. I now recognise and accept I created these dramas! I had a choice in who I dated! How ironic that when things went wrong, I would say things like, 'why is this happening to me?', when it was me who made these choices.

I also learned I was attracting the drama because I craved attention. At that time I wasn't willing to see that there is good attention and bad! I can now say:

"The biggest relationship I had to overcome was the one I had with myself."

Through years of bullying and continuing to treat myself like rubbish, I would be far too hard on myself and put myself down for the slightest thing. I was in a place of self-sabotaging, having no respect for myself and no self-worth.

I can honestly say:

"The hardest battle I have ever had to face was the one within me."

The relationship I had with my counsellor allowed me to build trust in people and overcome the fear of being criticised and judged.

Those regular weekly sessions showed me a different type of relationship. It proved to me that a person could be consistent, non-judgemental and loving.

I felt valued because she listened to my needs, and as a result I learned how to value myself.

What really stands out in my memory was how she listened to me. She listened to me without judgement or expectation, and with unconditional love. This kind of listening allowed the real me to shine through. I learned how to listen properly to myself. As a result:

'I learned how to have a good relationship with myself.'

I will never forget the relationship I had with my counsellor. I am truly grateful for the love and understanding I felt in those sessions.

As a counsellor now, it is a privilege to be able to give this kind of relationship to others. To give back what was given to me. To be able to give unconditional love.

The fact is that we all have a part to play in our relationships.

> During my teenage years I didn't like my mum. I was bitter towards her. This bitterness didn't help anybody. As I got older and was going through therapy, I learned to understand my mother. I became more accepting and my attitude towards my mother changed. As a result her attitude towards me changed.

When it comes to people's behaviour in relationships, don't always assume people know what they are doing, because most of the time they don't! It is important you vocalise if you feel you are being treated unfairly.

For example, some humour revolves around 'put down' humour. Some of this is fine, however it can get personal and hurt people's feelings. It is important that when things don't feel right that you communicate this. When 'put down' humour is used it is often meant as a bit of fun, but if it's not fun for you then you can use your voice and make people aware of this.

> When experiencing this in the past, I was told that I couldn't take a joke or that I was too sensitive. In other words, the person did not want to take responsibility for their behaviour. If people care about you, they will take on board what you have said, as they won't intentionally want to hurt you.

Some relationships are not meant to be. I have a better relationship with myself now, so I don't put up with the bad behaviour that I would have put up with in the past. I can recognise when someone is not in a good place, even if they are convinced that they are!

As mentioned earlier:

'It can be very difficult for people to be happy for you when they are not happy within themselves.'

If someone is not happy, they can come from a place of unhealthy emotions and may have a mind-set fuelled by bitterness and anger. They may mean well, but often they can project their negativity onto you without realising it. As a result, they may unconsciously bring you down and drain you of your energy.

If you have an honest relationship, you might be able to make the person aware of their behaviour. If you plan to do this, I would recommend putting a lot of thought into how you want to voice this, as the person is probably already feeling insecure and scared behind his or her negative behaviour. Speak to them from a place of love and understanding, and make sure that you are not coming across as 'having a go'. Ensure that they know it's because you value them and your relationship, and you only want what's best.

Be open to hear what they want to say, and be ready to listen to some truths about you that you may not like. Trust that you all mean well and that a lot of the time people don't intentionally want to hurt each other.

When you come from a place of love, if the person takes offence, then you know they are not ready to face their issues. This is their choice. Give them time.

If this is a family member or someone that you don't want to walk away from, then I encourage you to think about what you will, and will not put up with.

If the person is unwilling to look at their bad behaviour and is continuously disrespecting you, you can limit the time you spend with them. You can also look at other options like relationship counselling or a mediation service to find some common ground and healthy boundaries. All you can do is voice your concerns and be willing to look at your behaviour too.

If there is no change, over time this may become a relationship you feel you have to move away from, to protect your own mental health. Recognise you do have a choice.

I encourage you to trust your gut instinct with relationships, as this lets you know whether you are being treated fairly or not. It is important that you are aware of unhealthy relationships and the impact on you.

Being in a good relationship allows you to be open and honest with each other. You can do this because you are both looking out for each other's best interests.

For me, I had to communicate to my family about my depression, to make them aware of how their negative behaviour had affected me in the past, how they can support me now, and to create healthy boundaries to maintain my wellbeing.

In my experience, the majority of people mean well, want what's best for you and are not aware of how they are sometimes coming across. You can:

'Be the change you want in your relationships.'

CHAPTER 18

Meeting Your Needs

Everyone has needs and it is important to take time out to listen and find out what your personal needs are.

You might have social needs, which include doing social activities. This could be a hobby or interest like creative activities, dancing, sport or playing an instrument.

It's important to think about your health needs, and how they can be met like playing a sport and physical activities.

You may have financial needs to support the life you want.

You may have family needs, such as if you want to have children or be part of a family orientated community.

It is important that you take time out to meet your relaxation needs, including taking holidays and having fun. This is where work and life balance is important.

It is important for you to recognise your emotional needs. You may want to be in a stable relationship. To have friends that encourage and support you. To give love and be loved. To find out what your needs are, ask yourself:

Meeting your needs

In the past how have I met...

My social needs? (friends, family, relationships)

My creative needs? (hobbies and interests)

My health needs? (diet and exercise)

My emotional needs? (love in your life, offloading negativity)

My financial needs? (financial goals)

My work needs? (support, training, etc)

My relaxation and fun needs?

Do I have any...

Spiritual needs? (faith, religion, etc.)

Educational needs?

Aspirational needs? (capabilities and goals)

Are there any other needs that are important to me?

Whatever your needs are, it is important you take responsibility for yourself to find ways to meet them. This also involves finding out what makes you happy. As one of my clients said in one of our sessions:

'I owe it to myself to find out what makes me happy.'

This is true, and it's important that you do find out for yourself what makes you happy, and not expect other people to do it for you. When you expect other people to do it for you, you give your own personal power away. It also makes it easier to blame someone else when it doesn't work out for you. I encourage you to think about your needs, have fun making them happen and enjoy making yourself happier.

> **Meeting my emotional needs**
>
> As for meeting my own emotional needs, I am aware there is a need in me to be told I am loved. As mentioned before, I totally accept that vocally expressing love is difficult for my mum, so I found a healthy way to fulfil that gap. I have a beautiful friend, who is a similar age to my mum, who tells me she loves me all time. She understands my need to be told I am loved and gives me unconditional love whenever I need it.
>
> I also have a partner who tells he loves me all the time too.

I encourage you to let people in! Communicate your needs and find healthy ways to get them met!

CHAPTER 19

Support

I used to have difficulty accepting support, and sometimes still do. I know this is because of my deep-rooted conditioning to 'just get on with it', believing I have to do it on my own and that support isn't an option.

Believing this sort of conditioning is another way of ignoring your needs. If you can relate to this, then you can break free from this by challenging these beliefs and allowing support into your life.

In my business, I'm now building an effective support network of fellow professionals instead of trying to do everything myself.

We all need support!

In a counselling session, my client was complaining about a particular woman at work. She disliked her so much that I sensed there was more behind this, so asked her what it was about this woman that really bothered her. In exploration, it turned out that this woman was getting support at work and my client wasn't. My client had been conditioned not to ask for help, and as a result she was not meeting her needs and heading for a burn-out. After building this awareness we explored her options about what she could do differently. My client was then able to fulfil her own support needs, and as a result she no longer had issues with this woman!

Sometimes if you really don't like someone ask yourself:

'Is she or he getting something that I'm not?'

Again, we all need support. You don't have to be on your own. It is important you find the right people to give you the support you may need.

As an adult you are responsible for the life you lead.

**'You have 24 hours in a day until the day you die.
What you choose to do with it is down to you.'**

CHAPTER 20

Counselling Support

Thankfully, times have changed and there is a lot of counselling support available. If you are suffering from deep depression and need to talk to someone straight away then there are organisations out there, such as 'The Samaritans', where you can instantly talk to someone who cares.

If you want to find outside help with your relationships then I would recommend a counselling agency like 'Relate', who specialise in dealing with couples and family relationships.

If you want to deal with any deep-rooted personal issues then I would highly recommend counselling.

Always make sure you seek out a qualified professional to give you the help you may need.

There is a website called 'The Counselling Directory' which may help you with your search.

Be aware that the title of 'counsellor' can be widely used, and some coaches and mentors may not be qualified to deal with issues like deep depression and suicidal intent.

As a qualified counsellor, I work by a code of ethics set by the B.A.C.P. (The British Association of Counsellors and Psychotherapists). I set up a company called 'Mind Management For You' to ensure that clients get a professional service to meet their individual needs.

It can be helpful to know that there are different types of counselling models. The counselling I do is a mix of Person Centred, Gestalt, T.A. (Transaction Analysis) and C.B.T. (Cognitive Behavioural Therapy). I feel very fortunate that I have trained in different types of counselling which means I can tailor the counselling model to suit the individual.

C.B.T. Cognitive Behavioural Therapy counselling is solution focused and very good if you have surface issues or bad habits that you want to change by reframing your thinking.

If you have deep-rooted issues then I would recommend Person Centred, T.A., Gestalt or Psychodynamic Therapy to help you move forward.

Through counselling, I have made sense of my own upbringing and come up with my own solutions to move forward. This is very much what the counselling process is like.

First and foremost, it's about trust. The client has to feel they connect with and trust their counsellor. If not, they are well within their rights to ask to see someone else.

If it is 'Person Centred' counselling or 'client lead' counselling then the next stage is awareness. This involves the client offloading their issues to become more aware of the impact of them. Offloading allows the anger, sadness, guilt or whatever emotions are buried inside, to come out in a healthy way. When clients realise the impact past experiences have had on them, it can motivate them to want to change. Counselling gives them the space, encouragement and unconditional love to come up with their own solutions.

It's exciting times as new therapies are constantly being developed. However, there can be a period of trial and error until you find the right counselling model, and right therapist to suit you.

As humans we are always changing, and life is always changing so we never know what's going to happen next! I highlight this because as mentioned at the start of the book, when I went into counselling in my 20's I had the belief that once I'd done 3 to 6 months of counselling, or however long it took, then I'd be sorted for life! Hindsight, personal experiences and working with clients has taught me this is not always the case! Some people just need one group of sessions and that's it.

Others, like me, find that when life produces new challenges then some extra therapeutic support is needed to keep the old past conditioning in tow!

This happened when I recruited a personal assistant (P.A.). The self-sabotager in me had issues with me taking on a P.A. as I was struggling to believe I deserved to have one. Having these thoughts and feelings were making me feel worthless. I recognised the signs and had some therapy sessions to challenge the self-sabotaging thoughts that were holding me back! Nowadays the 'managing your thoughts' daily tracker keeps me in check. However I am open to extra counselling support whenever I need it.

I also believe timing has a very important part to play when it comes to receiving counselling help. When clients come to counselling they have to want to do it. They have to want to change. It can take tremendous courage for someone to admit they need help. They can be led by the conditioning that to ask for help is a sign of weakness when actually it takes courage and strength. Also, they may not be ready to face up to issues from the past.

'I believe we are all work in progress.'

Triggers can happen when you least expect them. It's important to recognise them, listen to your needs and be open to ask for help during the difficult times in your life.

Reading personal development books can be of great help in providing self support, and there is lots of different information that relates to most circumstances. There are plenty of personal development books out there, so I encourage you to have fun finding out what works for you!

CHAPTER 21

Living With Purpose

I encourage you to live with purpose. People can change over time, their priorities can change and what felt important in the past might not be as important now. For example, you may have a job that once felt right for you, but as time has passed you may feel bored and ready for a change. Living with purpose is living with passion. Passion in your work, your hobbies, your relationships and your achievements. The things that make you feel alive and make you want to do more!

Ask yourself:

> **When you wake up in the morning are you doing what you want to be doing?**
>
>
>
> **Are you excited about the day ahead?**

If the answer to the previous exercise is 'no' or 'not really', then I encourage you to claim your personal power and to try different things to find out what feels right for you. If your job is serving your financial needs and you are not in a position to change it, then I encourage you to acknowledge what needs your job is fulfilling and to be grateful for this. Then I encourage you to try new hobbies and interests to add more variety and passion to your life.

Even if you don't know what you want to do, you can have fun trying out new things! In my experience:

'Not doing anything can make you feel helpless.'

I heard a saying that the definition of madness is doing the same thing every day and expecting different results! If you are not happy with your life, you have the power and choice to do something about it.

There are many ways you can help yourself. You can help yourself by reading stories about other people in a similar situation to yours, and find out what they did to help themselves. Then you can do research on all the different options and opportunities that are out there.

You can believe that you have amazing capabilities and that you can achieve what you want.

You can research affirmations on the internet and decide what affirmations you can say to move you forward in the direction you want.

You can read about goal-setting and the different ways to make goals happen.

You can find people who want to help you. In my experience:

'There are loads of people who want to help you - all you have to do is ask.'

You can find people that inspire you. People that are living the life that you would like.

Then ask yourself:

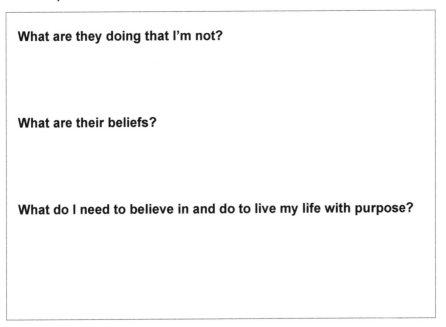

What are they doing that I'm not?

What are their beliefs?

What do I need to believe in and do to live my life with purpose?

Don't limit yourself by thinking 'it's too late', I'm past it.' Be kind to yourself and remember everyone has issues and insecurities around trying new things. Have realistic expectations in your capabilities, but be open and aware of the many things you can do. Besides,

**'How do you know you are not good at
something if you haven't tried it first?'**

Confidence and self-worth is built from beliefs and challenges – mainly the belief that **you can do it**, which comes from achievements and proving to yourself that you can do more.

Listen to your gut instinct. It will lead the way every time!!

CHAPTER 22

Unconditional Love

I mentioned at the start of the book that in an ideal world children would be brought up with unconditional love[11]. As mentioned, it can be difficult for parents or role models to give unconditional love if it was never shown to them in the first place. I learned what unconditional love was through counselling. I learned how to really apply it to myself through my counselling training. Not everybody wants to be a counsellor or go to counselling, but everyone deserves unconditional love.

For me, learning to love myself unconditionally was easier said than done! I had to believe that I deserved to be loved. That took time and a lot of scraping myself off the floor. Ironically I had to hit rock bottom first. I was absolutely sick of feeling like rubbish, always putting myself down and I was desperate to change. At that time I didn't know that my biggest issue was being unable to love myself unconditionally. All I knew was what I was doing wasn't working. I needed help, and when I allowed myself to see my own vulnerability, things started to change.

11. Sue Gerhardt – 'Why love matters'

When you learn to love yourself unconditionally you see yourself in a different light. You open up to your capabilities and you allow yourself to grow without judgements, expectations, fear or criticism.

When you come from a place of unconditional love you accept that you are human and that it's ok to get things wrong. You let go of unrealistic expectations and accept who you are.

I encourage you to love yourself unconditionally. Be less hard on yourself and have more fun!

CHAPTER 23

Enjoying The Journey

I hope the exercises in this book have helped you to get to know yourself better. By building your awareness, you may increase your confidence in learning what makes you happy, gaining more clarity about what your needs are, so you can work towards meeting your needs to live a fulfilled life.

At the end of the day everyone just wants to be loved. Everyone has insecurities.

> I remember in primary school when I was about 11 years old, there was a good looking girl who all the boys fancied. All the girls were jealous of her. From the outside it looked like she had everything – great looks, lots of attention and loads of boys around her. One day I asked her what it was like to be so good looking and popular. She told me that most days she hated her good looks. I was surprised! I asked why and she said it was because the boys didn't care about her as a person, and girls were always comparing themselves to her, so she found it hard to maintain real friendships.

So you see, regardless of looks, wealth or circumstances, everybody has issues. There is no point comparing yourself to other people. Happiness is what really matters.

'Focus on what makes you happy and you will be so happy doing what you love that you won't care what others think!'

I encourage you to love yourself unconditionally, without judgements, expectations and self-limiting beliefs. To love yourself with pure acceptance, so you can accept your faults and learn from them. Trust that you come from a good place and that you are doing your best. Trust and know that you are enough, just as you are.

Recognise your own power and that you have choices. Open your heart to the wonderful opportunities that are around you and just go for it! Go for it without any fear or worries about what others think. Just trust, enjoy and discover your own capabilities.

Personal summary

Writing this book has been a very insightful and emotional journey. It has increased my understanding and allowed me to let go of things I was unconsciously holding on to in the past. As a result I am now free. Free from the negative conditioning that has held me back for years. Free from the constant feelings of worthlessness and beliefs that I didn't deserve to be loved. I honestly feel like I have been born again – but this time without the negative conditioning holding me back.

I now know I have the ability to make the most of what I have got. I now see how all of us are equal and deserve the life we want. I now know my life can be as good as I choose and allow it to be. I am free to make positive choices. I can continue to enjoy becoming the best comedienne that I can be, giving myself every opportunity to discover my potential.

So, bring it on! I see life as a gift. Everyday just as precious as the next. I'm mindful of the fact that one day I won't be here so, boy, am I going to enjoy the ride!

'I see my life as a journey and I'm just enjoying the ride.'

I feel certain that I can handle whatever life throws at me. I will not be afraid to ask for support and I certainly won't feel guilty about it! I will take full responsibility for my actions and accept I am not perfect. I understand that sometimes I will get it wrong and that's ok.

I am now ready to move into the next chapter of my life. Ready to use all I have learned in the past to create the now. I am determined to turn my negative past into a positive future and to continue to help others, along with freeing myself of any victim mentality. I intend to be present in my world - to just be.

I am excited about what the future holds for me, and can tell you that one of my goals is have my own mental health show on TV. I want to reduce the stigma around mental health and educate people. I want to spread the learning, the unconditional love, and use humour to show how:

'Life is too serious to be taken seriously.'

I want to interview the experts, talk openly about depression and show how we are all nuts in our own way, but mainly how we can all help ourselves and each other.

I don't know how I'm going to have my own show on TV, but just like the way I left Ireland 13 years ago, not knowing how I was going to be an entertainer, I'm just going to go for it and make it happen. To trust that, like before, the 'how' will sort itself out.

I will continue to enjoy the privilege of counselling people on a one-to-one basis, giving talks and hosting workshops. My clients have given me more than great testimonials, as by helping them, they have also helped me.

My life is now an open book. I have nothing to hide and so much to give. For the first time in my life I can honestly say:

"I believe in me."

I hope this book will help you on your life journey and I welcome your feedback. If I can help in anyway, please do get in touch.

I wish you a fulfilled and happy life.

Love,
Sheila

USEFUL LINKS

www.mind.org.uk
www.samaritans.org
www.relate.org.uk
www.time-to-change.org.uk

ACKNOWLEDGEMENTS

I would like to thank all the people who have helped me to make this book happen. My counselling supervisor, past and present clients and especially clients who have given me their permission to use their feedback in this book so that it may be of benefit to others.

I would like to thank my partner who was there for me during the emotional process of writing this book.

Thank you to my friends for your support and for the encouragement I needed.

Thank you to my investor who believes in me and this book.

Thank you to my own therapist who helped me make sense of my world when I felt lost.

Thank you to my faith in God that has kept me going through all the tough times.

Thank you to my family, for sharing their experiences and honesty.

Finally, I would like to thank you for taking time out to read this book. I hope for some of you it has empowered you to fulfil your own needs and enjoy creating a life full of abundance.

NOTES

NOTES

NOTES

Lightning Source UK Ltd.
Milton Keynes UK
UKHW02f1525130418

321019UK00006B/216/P